FOCUS ON CURRENT EVENTS
VACCINES
by Matt Chandler

FOCUS READERS®
VOYAGER

www.focusreaders.com

Copyright © 2022 by Focus Readers®, Lake Elmo, MN 55042. All rights reserved. No part of this book may be reproduced or utilized in any form or by any means without written permission from the publisher.

Focus Readers is distributed by North Star Editions:
sales@northstareditions.com | 888-417-0195

Produced for Focus Readers by Red Line Editorial.

Content Consultant: Stephanie Perniciaro, PhD, MPH, Associate Research Scientist in Epidemiology of Microbial Diseases, Yale School of Public Health

Photographs ©: Shutterstock Images, cover, 1, 7, 8–9, 11, 13, 14–15, 17, 19, 22–23, 24, 27, 28–29, 30, 33, 34–35, 39, 40–41, 43; AP Images, 4–5; iStockphoto, 21; Red Line Editorial, 37, 44

Library of Congress Cataloging-in-Publication Data
Names: Chandler, Matt, author.
Title: Vaccines / by Matt Chandler.
Description: Lake Elmo, MN : Focus Readers, [2022] | Series: Focus on current events | Includes index. | Audience: Grades 4-6
Identifiers: LCCN 2021041278 (print) | LCCN 2021041279 (ebook) | ISBN 9781637390801 (hardcover) | ISBN 9781637391341 (paperback) | ISBN 9781637391884 (ebook) | ISBN 9781637392355 (pdf)
Subjects: LCSH: Vaccines--Juvenile literature. | Vaccination--Juvenile literature.
Classification: LCC RA638 .C535 2022 (print) | LCC RA638 (ebook) | DDC 615.3/72--dc23
LC record available at https://lccn.loc.gov/2021041278
LC ebook record available at https://lccn.loc.gov/2021041279

Printed in the United States of America
Mankato, MN
012022

ABOUT THE AUTHOR

Matt Chandler is the author of more than 75 books for children. His book *Side-by-Side Baseball Stars* was named Best Children's Book of 2015 by the American Society of Journalists and Authors (ASJA). Matt lives in New York with his wife and children.

TABLE OF CONTENTS

CHAPTER 1
Dr. Salk Changes the World 5

CHAPTER 2
The History of Vaccines 9

CHAPTER 3
How Vaccines Work 15

CASE STUDY
The Other Polio Vaccine 20

CHAPTER 4
Developing a Vaccine 23

CHAPTER 5
Vaccine Access 29

CASE STUDY
Immunizing Children 32

CHAPTER 6
COVID-19 35

CHAPTER 7
Vaccine Controversy 41

Focus on Vaccines • 46
Glossary • 47
To Learn More • 48
Index • 48

CHAPTER 1

DR. SALK CHANGES THE WORLD

On March 26, 1953, Dr. Jonas Salk made a major announcement on national radio. He had created a vaccine to protect against polio. In 1952 alone, more than 58,000 Americans had been diagnosed with this disease. Most were children, and more than 3,000 died from it.

Polio is caused by a **virus** that attacks a person's muscles and spinal cord. People with polio may struggle to walk. They may wear braces

Dr. Jonas Salk studied viruses to create a vaccine for polio.

5

on their legs. Or they may need wheelchairs. Polio can also attack the muscles used for breathing.

As a result, some patients needed machines called iron lungs. These machines pressed air in and out of patients' chests. A large metal tube surrounded each patient's body. Only his or her head stuck out. Because polio could have such serious consequences, many people feared the disease.

Salk tested his vaccine during the early 1950s. Children under age five were most at risk to catch polio. So, the tests involved young children. Thousands of children received doses of Salk's vaccine. Doctors then examined the children to make sure the vaccine worked and was safe. They looked for signs of sickness or other problems.

In 1955, Salk's vaccine was approved for public use. Long lines often formed outside clinics.

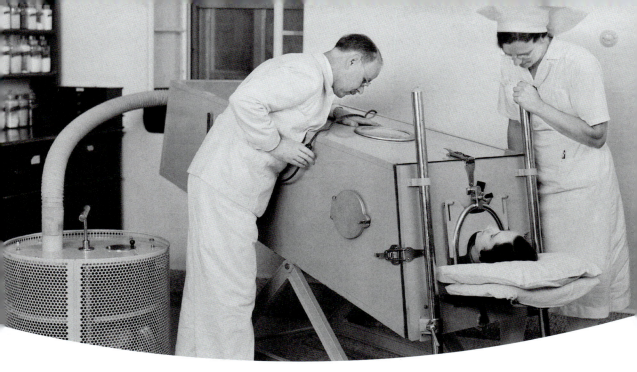

▲ Some patients used iron lungs for a few weeks. Others needed the machines for the rest of their lives.

Many families were eager to get the polio vaccine. Soon, millions of children had received it. By 1957, the number of polio cases in the United States had dropped to 6,000.

A second polio vaccine was created in 1960. It was soon used around the world. Thanks to these vaccines, polio outbreaks became much less common.

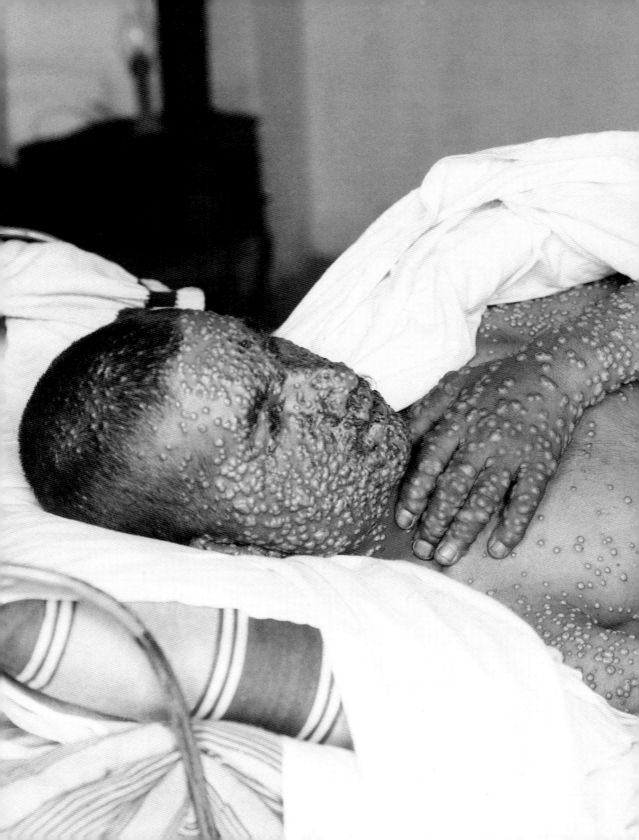

CHAPTER 2

THE HISTORY OF VACCINES

Most medicines cure a disease or treat its symptoms. A vaccine helps prevent a person from getting sick in the first place. It does this by helping the person's body develop a defense against a disease.

The first disease that a vaccine helped prevent was smallpox. This disease caused painful sores on the skin. It spread very quickly. And it killed 30 percent of people who got it.

Before a vaccine was created, smallpox was one of the deadliest diseases in history.

People in Africa and Asia used **inoculation** to prevent it. A small part of a smallpox sore was put into a person's skin. Then, that person wouldn't get sick. In 1796, Dr. Edward Jenner used this method to make a vaccine. He noticed that people who had gotten a less-serious disease called cowpox didn't get smallpox. So, he took liquid from cowpox sores. He put it in small cuts on people's arms. These people became immune to smallpox. They didn't catch the disease.

Scientists began using similar methods to make other vaccines. One of these scientists was Louis Pasteur. In 1885, he helped create a vaccine

➤ THINK ABOUT IT

How might preventing a disease be more helpful than treating its symptoms?

▲ Louis Pasteur's work on the rabies vaccine helped scientists understand how germs caused diseases.

for rabies. He also learned about how diseases spread. He found they were caused by tiny germs. This knowledge helped scientists make vaccines for other diseases.

Many important vaccines were developed during the 1900s. One was for typhoid fever. Several typhoid outbreaks took place in the early 1900s. Then a vaccine became available in 1914. Typhoid became rare in most developed countries.

Many vaccines helped prevent diseases that affected children. These diseases often spread quickly and could be fatal. A vaccine for diphtheria was released in 1926. Before this vaccine, diphtheria was a leading cause of childhood death. In the 1930s, a whooping cough vaccine saved even more children's lives.

The tetanus vaccine was also important. Tetanus attacks muscles and nerves. People who catch it may become unable to breathe. There was no cure for tetanus. But a vaccine became available in 1938.

Vaccines for measles, mumps, and rubella were created in the 1960s. These diseases spread quickly. Plus, they could cause serious health problems in young children. In 1964 and 1965, a rubella outbreak happened in the United States. More than 12 million people were infected.

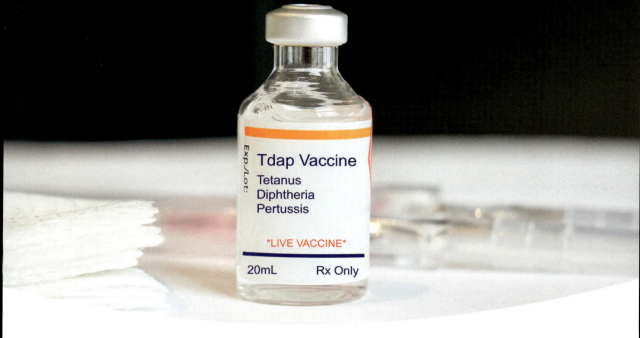

▲ The Tdap vaccine became available in 2005. It helps prevent tetanus, diphtheria, and whooping cough.

Thousands of babies died. But thanks to vaccines, cases became rare. In 1971, the MMR (measles, mumps, and rubella) vaccine came out. It helped protect against all three diseases at once.

Since 2000, vaccines have been created for even more diseases. Scientists continue researching new vaccines. By preventing illness, vaccines can save millions of lives.

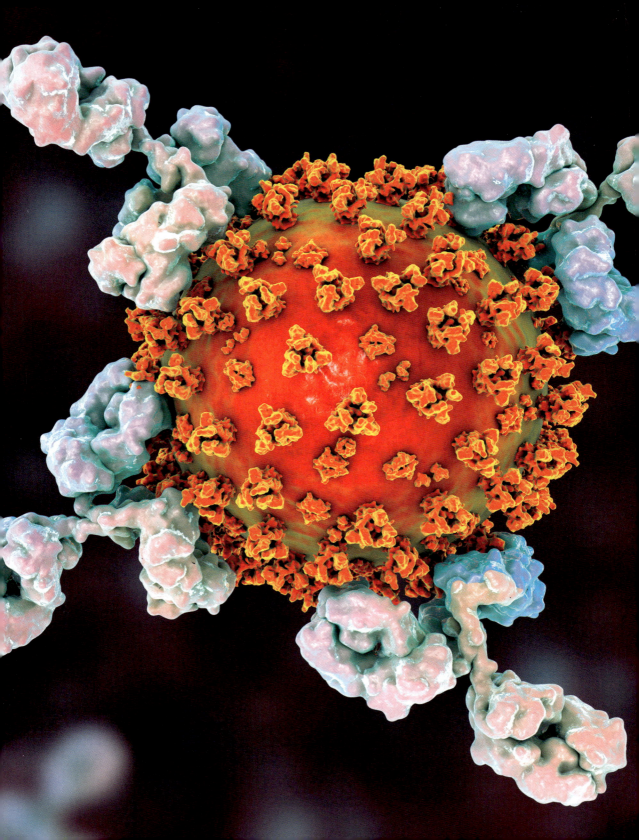

CHAPTER 3

HOW VACCINES WORK

Vaccines work by helping a person's body fight off germs. These germs can be viruses or **bacteria**. There are several different types of vaccines. An inactivated vaccine uses a sample of a germ that has been killed. When the vaccine enters a person's body, the **immune system** reacts to the dead germ. It creates antibodies. Antibodies are **proteins** created by the body to protect against sickness. They recognize and

Antibodies (white) fight infections by attaching themselves to germs (red).

15

attack certain germs. If these germs enter the body later on, the antibodies can fight them off. Vaccines for influenza, polio, and rabies use inactivated viruses.

A live-attenuated vaccine includes a tiny amount of a live germ. This germ is weakened to prevent it from making the person sick. Instead, the person's body produces antibodies for the disease. Fighting the weak germ is more like fighting the real disease. So, this method often produces stronger antibodies than an inactivated vaccine does. However, not everyone can get live vaccines. People with weak immune systems may

THINK ABOUT IT

Why might it be helpful for scientists to create so many different types of vaccines?

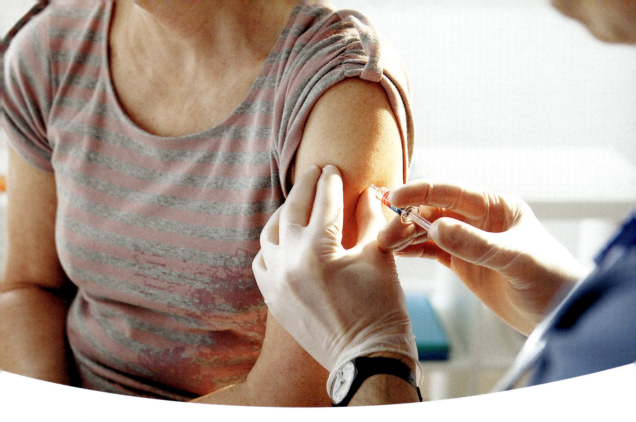

▲ Shingles is a disease that mainly affects people over the age of 50. A subunit vaccine helps prevent it.

not be able to fight off the weak germs. Vaccines for smallpox and chickenpox use this method.

Subunit vaccines use just part of a virus or bacteria. This part may be a coating that goes around the germ. Or it may be a protein the germ uses. The vaccine trains the body to recognize and attack this piece. By targeting one piece, the immune system can destroy the whole germ. In many cases, it can also make a stronger attack. This type of vaccine is used for typhoid, shingles, and HPV.

Toxoid vaccines use a similar method. They prevent diseases caused by bacteria. Bacteria often make people sick by producing a toxin. This substance harms the body's cells. A toxoid vaccine includes a weakened version of this toxin. It trains the body to identify and fight it. If the bacteria enter the body, the body will attack the parts of them that make the toxin. The tetarus vaccine is a toxoid vaccine.

A viral vector vaccine uses a modified version of a virus. This version trains the body how to fight a different disease. The modified virus is called a vector. Ebola vaccines use this method. So do some COVID-19 vaccines.

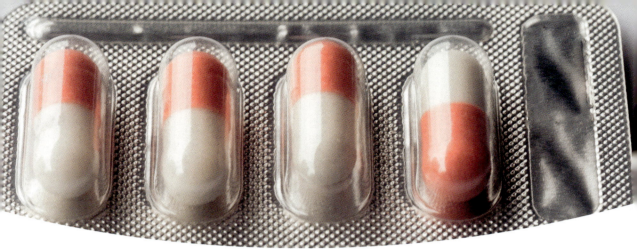

▲ For the oral typhoid vaccine, people swallow a series of pills. After that, immunity lasts for five years.

An mRNA vaccine doesn't use any part of the virus. Instead, it causes the body to create proteins. These proteins help the immune system fight off the virus. Some COVID-19 vaccines are this type.

Many vaccines are given as shots. Others are taken orally as pills or drops. After some vaccines, immunity lasts for the rest of the person's life. For other vaccines, immunity wears off over time. People may need booster shots to stay protected. These shots give extra doses of the vaccine.

CASE STUDY

THE OTHER POLIO VACCINE

Dr. Salk's polio vaccine was an inactivated vaccine. It had a small amount of dead poliovirus in it. Dr. Albert Sabin created a live-attenuated polio vaccine. His vaccine used a small amount of live poliovirus. Using a live virus can give people stronger antibodies. That can lead to better protection. Immunity can last longer, too. People often need multiple doses of inactivated vaccines. But many active vaccines protect people for the rest of their lives.

For Salk's vaccine, people needed three shots. Sabin's vaccine required four doses. It used drops that went in people's mouths. Sabin thought that children would more easily take a vaccine they could swallow. He was right. His oral vaccine was used in the United States and around the

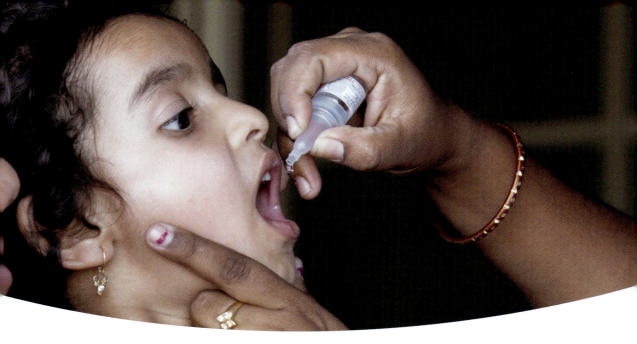

▲ The oral polio vaccine helped significantly lower the number of polio cases in many countries.

world. It helped eliminate polio from the Western Hemisphere.

However, live vaccines have some additional risks. A small number of patients may get sick from the vaccine. In rare cases, patients who got Sabin's vaccine developed polio. Because of this, the United States stopped using live-virus polio vaccines in 2000. Some other countries continued to use this type of polio vaccine. But by the 2020s, it was being phased out.

CHAPTER 4

DEVELOPING A VACCINE

Creating a vaccine often takes years and costs millions of dollars. There are six main steps in the development process. First, scientists and doctors do research and experiments. They focus on a specific disease. They work to find an **antigen** that will help fight the disease. The antigen may be a toxin or a part of a germ. It triggers the immune system.

It may take scientists 10 to 15 years to develop a vaccine.

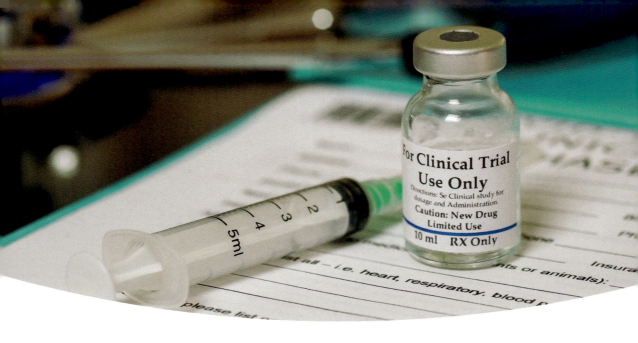

▲ Clinical trials are part of the clinical development stage.

Next, scientists test how the antigen works. Scientists often use animals for these tests. The tests help them learn how the human body might respond. This preclinical stage is where many vaccines fail. They might not show the ability to produce the correct antibodies. Those vaccines are not approved.

The next stage of the process is clinical development. This stage has three phases.

In Phase I, a small group of people are given the vaccine. Researchers watch them to see how they react. If anyone gets sick, the symptoms are recorded and studied. Researchers then try to find ways to make the vaccine safer.

Phase II involves a much larger number of people. One group in this phase receives the vaccine. This phase also includes a placebo group. Members of this group don't get the vaccine. But they don't know this. Researchers compare the symptoms of these two groups. This step helps show if the vaccine made a difference.

Phase III repeats the testing with even more people. Thousands of patients receive the vaccine. This large number is important. Vaccines may have **side effects** that only show up in a small percentage of people. With thousands of people, it's easier to see if any side effects will develop.

After Phase III, clinical development is complete. Then, the company submits its vaccine for regulatory review. In the United States, vaccines are approved by the Food and Drug Administration (FDA). The FDA looks at the results of the clinical studies. It decides whether to issue a license to produce the vaccine.

If a vaccine is approved, manufacturing can begin. Drug companies produce the vaccine in huge amounts. Then the vaccine is shipped to doctors, hospitals, and clinics. At that point, it can be given to patients.

Quality control is the last step. Scientists and doctors continue to test the vaccine to make sure it's safe. They also monitor the results from people who receive it. They look for side effects or other problems. For example, some of the vaccine's ingredients could be **contaminated**.

▲ In the United States, the FDA reviews vaccines to make sure they are safe and effective.

If problems appear, the vaccine may be pulled off the market. Scientists try to find out what caused the problems. They decide if the vaccine can be safe enough to use again or if it must be permanently stopped. In 2021, for instance, a few patients developed blood clots after getting the Johnson & Johnson COVID-19 vaccine. After a review, the vaccine was found to be safe overall. People could continue using it.

CHAPTER 5

VACCINE ACCESS

Thanks to vaccines, several deadly diseases have been **eradicated**. Others have become very rare. However, millions of people around the world are unable to get vaccines. As a result, more than 1.5 million people die from preventable diseases every year.

There are a variety of reasons for this. One reason is cost. Drug companies may charge high prices for their vaccines. Many people can't afford

Malaria kills thousands of children around the world each year. To help prevent this, Kenya launched a malaria vaccine program in 2019.

▲ Many vaccines must be stored inside refrigerators, coolers, or freezers.

them. This is especially true for people without medical insurance. Prices can affect entire countries, too. Wealthy countries can easily buy lots of vaccines. They often have more vaccines than they need. Meanwhile, low-income countries don't have enough.

Location can also be a problem. People must usually visit doctors or clinics to get vaccines. Some people don't own cars. Or they live in rural areas. The nearest clinic may be a long journey away.

In addition, some vaccines must be kept cold. This can make it challenging to deliver vaccines to people in remote areas. And in places that don't have reliable electricity, vaccines can be difficult to store.

People around the world are working to solve these problems. Some help create traveling vaccination clinics. They go directly to people living in rural communities. Other groups work on lowering the cost of vaccines. Some help create programs that offer free vaccines. Helping more people have access to vaccines will save millions of lives.

THINK ABOUT IT

What are some other reasons people might not receive vaccines? What could people or governments do to help solve these problems?

CASE STUDY

IMMUNIZING CHILDREN

Each year, approximately 20 million babies around the world don't get basic vaccines. Many of these babies live in low-income countries. In these places, people often face poverty and lack of medical care. For example, researchers estimate that, every year, more than 30 million children in Africa under the age of five suffer from a disease that a vaccine could have prevented.

Groups such as the Clinton Health Access Initiative (CHAI) hope to change this. CHAI works to help more people have access to medical care. As part of this work, it aims to increase the number of children being vaccinated each year.

CHAI helps countries get lower prices from vaccine companies. It also helps countries find ways to safely ship and store the doses.

▲ Regular access to medical care is a main factor in helping more children survive past age five.

In addition, CHAI partners with 11 countries in Africa and Asia. It supports their national vaccine programs. These programs typically give eight vaccines to babies. CHAI helped Kenya, Ethiopia, and Malawi add two more vaccines. This change is estimated to prevent 50,000 children from dying each year. Several other organizations do similar work around the world. Together, they try to help children get the health care they need to stay healthy and safe.

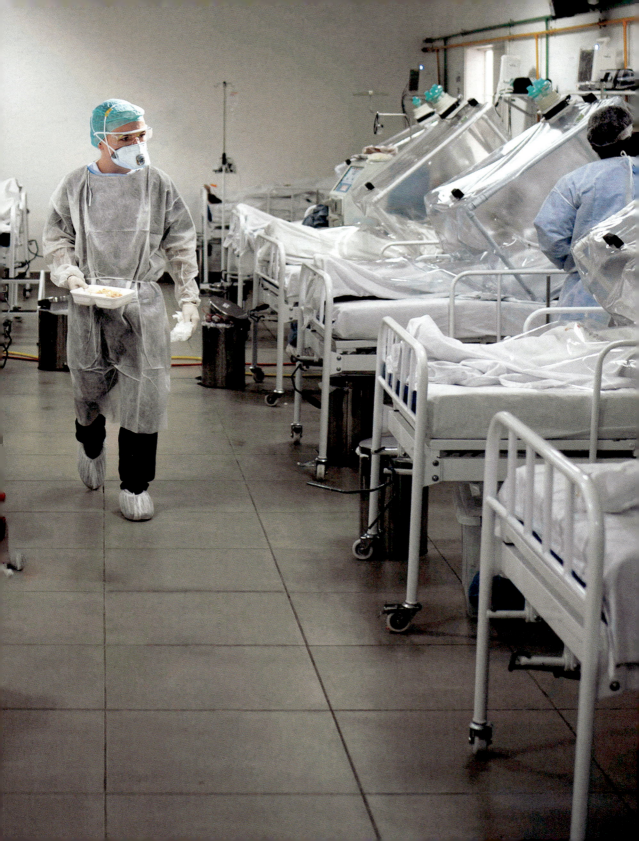

CHAPTER 6

COVID-19

Scientists continue to develop new vaccines. For example, COVID-19 began spreading around the world in early 2020. It quickly became the largest health threat in modern history. Nearly one million people died in the first six months of the pandemic. By mid-2021, more than four million lives had been lost.

Researchers raced to make a vaccine for the virus. It was a global effort. Countries worked

During the COVID-19 pandemic, a dangerous virus spread quickly around the world. Hospitals filled with seriously ill patients.

together. Scientists shared data. Some had worked on similar vaccines in the past. Multiple COVID-19 vaccines were being developed at the same time. The testing process went faster, too. Clinical trials often take two years. That's partly because it can take a long time to get volunteers. During the pandemic, however, people were eager to get COVID-19 vaccines. Volunteers quickly filled up the trials. Trials must also test whether vaccinated people can still get sick from the virus. Usually, it takes a long time for many people to be exposed to a virus. But COVID-19 spread extremely fast. Millions of people were exposed. So, testing didn't take as long as usual.

By early 2021, three COVID-19 vaccines had been approved for use in the United States. Companies began developing them in early 2020. All completed testing in record time. At first, the

COVID-19 vaccines were only for people ages 16 and up. Scientists did extra testing to make sure the vaccines were safe for children. By May 2021, the FDA had approved one of the vaccines for people as young as 12 years old.

The scientific evidence from the trials showed that the vaccines were safe. It also showed they were very effective at preventing severe illness

COVID-19 VACCINES IN THE UNITED STATES

Company	Vaccine Type	Doses	First Approved
Pfizer	mRNA	2 doses, 21 days apart	December 2020
Moderna	mRNA	2 doses, 28 days apart	December 2020
Johnson & Johnson	Viral vector	only 1 dose	February 2021

and death from COVID-19. However, a small number of people experienced health problems after receiving them. In addition, some online videos and articles incorrectly linked the vaccines to sickness or death. As a result, some people felt that the vaccines were too risky. These people chose not to get vaccinated. This choice could have serious consequences. In May 2021, more than 99 percent of people in the United States who died from COVID-19 were unvaccinated.

When a large percentage of people are immune to a disease, the disease can't spread as much. This concept is known as herd immunity. It's a key part of stopping contagious diseases. Vaccines often play an important role. People help protect themselves and others by getting vaccinated.

Experts studied herd immunity for COVID-19. They estimated that at least 70 percent of the

▲ Health care workers wore masks and face shields when giving COVID-19 vaccines to avoid spreading germs.

world's population would need to be vaccinated. By the fall of 2021, more than six billion doses of COVID-19 vaccines had been given across the globe. Still, some countries struggled to convince enough people to get vaccinated. And low-income countries often didn't have enough vaccines to give people. That left experts worried that COVID-19 would continue to infect and kill large numbers of people.

CHAPTER 7

VACCINE CONTROVERSY

Some people can't get vaccines for medical reasons. They may be allergic to an ingredient in a vaccine. Or they may have weak immune systems. If they receive a vaccine with a live germ in it, their bodies might not be able to fight the germ off. In addition, some people avoid vaccines because of their religious beliefs. Still others oppose vaccines because they claim vaccines cause health problems, especially in

Some people don't believe vaccines should be required.

children. These people are sometimes known as anti-vaxxers.

The anti-vaxxer movement was partly driven by a study released in 1997. In this study, a surgeon named Andrew Wakefield claimed to find a link between the MMR vaccine and autism. Wakefield's study was filled with mistakes. It was removed from the medical journal that published it. And Wakefield lost his medical license. Later studies showed no link between vaccines and autism. But some people still use this reasoning. Others believe that the germs or ingredients in vaccines are dangerous. Evidence shows that the risks are very low. Even so, some parents are still afraid to give their children vaccines.

Governments may require people to get certain vaccines. In 1853, the United Kingdom became the first country to make vaccines mandatory.

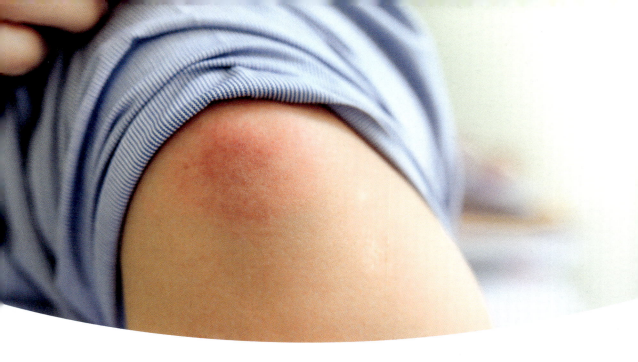

⚠ Some patients experience soreness or swelling after they get a vaccine. But most serious side effects are quite rare.

Many other countries followed. In the United States, for instance, vaccinations are required for all students at public schools. That said, most US states offer **exemptions** for religious or other reasons.

Some people say getting vaccines should be an individual choice. However, choosing not to get a vaccine doesn't just affect individuals.

Herd immunity depends on the actions of a large group. If fewer people get vaccines, diseases can spread more easily. This can have serious consequences.

For example, a measles outbreak took place in Minnesota in 2017. It affected an area where fewer

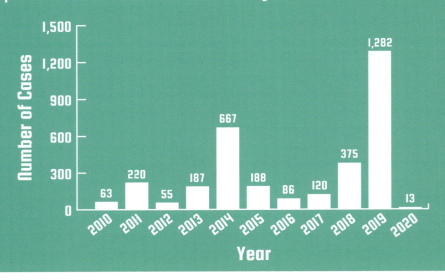

MEASLES CASES IN THE UNITED STATES

The US government tracks the number of measles cases reported in the United States each year.

people were vaccinated. Dozens of people got sick. More than 8,000 were exposed. Some had to stay home from work or school. And 22 people went to the hospital. If fewer people get vaccines, outbreaks like this can become more common.

In many cases, the choice not to vaccinate is based on fear. For instance, rumors spread about COVID-19 vaccines. Some said the vaccines included microchips that would track people. Others said the vaccines changed people's **DNA**. These claims were proven false. Even so, millions of people chose not to get COVID-19 vaccines.

However, huge numbers of people did get COVID-19 vaccines. That led to big drops in the number of people catching or dying from the virus. As a result, the pandemic began to slow in some places. Vaccines continue to play an important role in stopping the spread of disease.

FOCUS ON
VACCINES

Write your answers on a separate piece of paper.

1. Write a paragraph describing the steps used to develop a vaccine.

2. Do you think governments should require people to get certain vaccines? Why or why not?

3. Which disease did the first vaccine help prevent?
- **A.** smallpox
- **B.** tetanus
- **C.** COVID-19

4. Why would immunity from a live vaccine last longer than immunity from an inactivated vaccine?
- **A.** Inactivated vaccines don't include any parts of the actual virus.
- **B.** Live vaccines use a weakened virus, which can't trigger an immune response.
- **C.** Live vaccines use a weakened virus, which triggers a stronger immune response.

Answer key on page 48.

GLOSSARY

antigen
A foreign substance that a person's body tries to fight off.

bacteria
Microscopic, single-celled living things. Some bacteria cause disease, and some do not.

contaminated
Made dirty or unsafe by having something else mixed in.

DNA
The genetic material in the cells of living organisms.

eradicated
Gotten rid of completely.

exemptions
Permission to not do something that is usually required.

immune system
The body system that uses specialized cells to fight infections.

inoculation
Using a small amount of a disease to help a person's body build a defense against that disease and keep the person from getting sick.

proteins
Molecules that are important in telling a living cell what to do.

side effects
Reactions caused by taking a medicine or vaccine that are not part of what is supposed to happen.

virus
A tiny substance that can infect people or animals and cause disease.

TO LEARN MORE

BOOKS

Edwards, Sue Bradford. *Coronavirus: The COVID-19 Pandemic*. Minneapolis: Abdo Publishing, 2021.

Haelle, Tara. *Vaccination Investigation: The History and Science of Vaccines*. Minneapolis: Lerner Publishing, 2018.

Harris, Duchess, with Heather C. Hudak. *The Discovery of the Polio Vaccine*. Minneapolis: Abdo Publishing, 2019.

NOTE TO EDUCATORS

Visit **www.focusreaders.com** to find lesson plans, activities, links, and other resources related to this title.

INDEX

anti-vaxxer movement, 41–45

bacteria, 15, 17–18

COVID-19, 18–19, 27, 35–39, 45

germs, 11, 15–18, 23, 41–42

herd immunity, 38, 44

immune system, 15–19, 23, 41
inactivated vaccine, 15–16, 20–21

live-attenuated vaccine, 16, 20

mRNA vaccine, 19

polio, 5–7, 16, 20–21

research, 10–11, 13, 23–27, 32, 35–37

smallpox, 9–10, 17
subunit vaccine, 17

testing, 6, 24–27, 36–37
tetanus, 12, 18
toxoid vaccine, 18
typhoid, 11, 18

viral vector vaccine, 18
virus, 5, 15–19, 20–21, 35–45

Answer Key: 1. Answers will vary; 2. Answers will vary; 3. A; 4. C

48